CONTENTS

GETTING STARTED

Welcome to the world of a concept car designer. You'll get hands-on experience designing cars for big-time clients. Here are the tools to get you started.

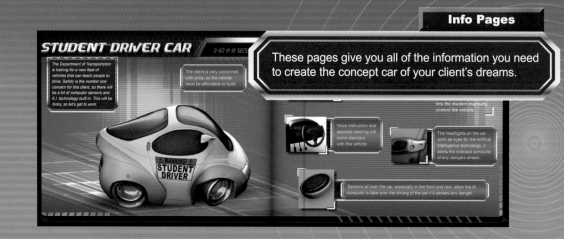

STUDENT DRIVER CAR 0-60 in 18 secs

The Department of Transportation is looking for a new fleet of vehicles that can teach people to drive. Safety is the number one concern for this client, so there will be a lot of computer sensors and A.I. technology built in. This will be tricky, so let's get to work.

The client is very concerned with price, so the vehicle must be affordable to build.

lets the student manually control the vehicle.

Voice instruction and assisted steering will come standard with this vehicle.

The headlights on the car work as eyes for the Artifical Intelligence technology. It alerts the onboard computer of any dangers ahead.

Sensors all over the car, especially in the front and rear, allow the AI computer to take over the driving of the car if it senses any danger.

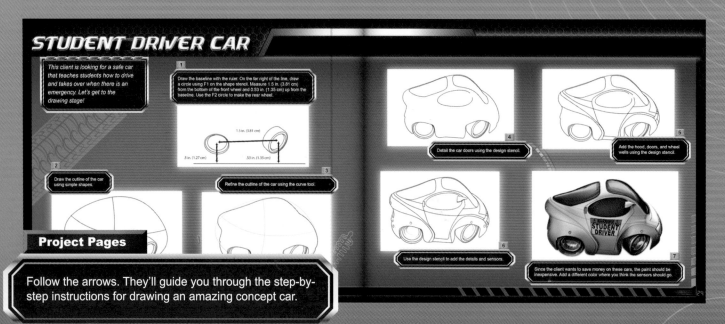

STUDENT DRIVER CAR

This client is looking for a safe car that teaches students how to drive and takes over when there is an emergency. Let's get to the drawing stage!

1. Draw the baseline with the ruler. On the far right of the line, draw a circle using F1 on the shape stencil. Measure 1.5 in. (3.81 cm) from the bottom of the front wheel and 0.53 in. (1.35 cm) up from the baseline. Use the F2 circle to make the rear wheel.

1.5 in. (3.81 cm)
.5 in. (1.27 cm)   .53 in. (1.35 cm)

2. Draw the outline of the car using simple shapes.

3. Refine the outline of the car using the curve tool.

4. Detail the car doors using the design stencil.

5. Add the hood, doors, and wheel wells using the design stencil.

6. Use the design stencil to add the details and sensors.

7. Since the client wants to save money on these cars, the paint should be inexpensive. Add a different color where you think the sensors should go.

Project Pages

Follow the arrows. They'll guide you through the step-by-step instructions for drawing an amazing concept car.

Step by Step

The projects are broken down into simple steps. Each step builds on the next from simple shapes to the finished car. You'll get all of the information you need and which tool to use to create an incredible car.

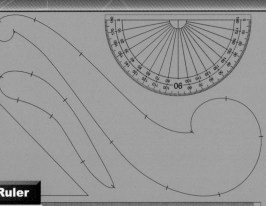

Ellipses, Curves, and Ruler

With this book, you got a ruler, curve, and circle template. Use these tools to refine edges, create the wheels, and make your car design look professional.

Colors

Each project ends with a finished sketch of the car in color. You can follow the color patterns exactly or you can create your own. Use your imagination. It's the best tool you've got!

WARNING!
STUDENT DRIVER

Design Stencil

LUXURY SEDAN

CHAMELEON CAR

TUTOR CAR

SPORTS CAR

ARTIFICIAL INTELLIGENCE

COUCH CAR

HOVER CAR

The design stencil will help you add detail to your concept car. It is divided into sections for each project.

LUXURY SEDAN

Your car-manufacturing client is looking for a Luxury Sedan that combines speed and luxury. It should have an array of features including a powerful engine, supercool rims, comfort, and the smooth ride of a sports car. Ready to give them what they want?

The car manufacturer is looking for class and comfort, so get drawing!

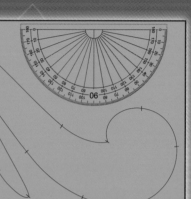

Step by Step

The projects are broken down into simple steps. Each step builds on the next from simple shapes to the finished car. You'll get all of the information you need and which tool to use to create an incredible car.

Ellipses, Curves, and Ruler

With this book, you got a ruler, curve, and circle template. Use these tools to refine edges, create the wheels, and make your car design look professional.

Colors

Each project ends with a finished sketch of the car in color. You can follow the color patterns exactly or you can create your own. Use your imagination. It's the best tool you've got!

STUDENT DRIVER

⚠ WARNING! ⚠

Design Stencil

LUXURY SEDAN

CHAMELEON CAR

TUTOR CAR

SPORTS CAR

ARTIFICIAL INTELLIGENCE

COUCH CAR

HOVER CAR

The design stencil will help you add detail to your concept car. It is divided into sections for each project.

0-60 IN 10 SECS.

Your car-manufacturing client is looking for a Luxury Sedan that combines speed and luxury. It should have an array of features including a powerful engine, supercool rims, comfort, and the smooth ride of a sports car. Ready to give them what they want?

The car manufacturer is looking for class and comfort, so get drawing!

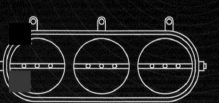

The client is looking for a special dashboard and steering wheel with controls at your fingertips.

According to the client, the passengers must ride in ultimate comfort, so add back massagers to all of the passengers seats.

The car's ride should be like gliding on silk, so make sure the suspension will give you that kind of ride.

Be sure to add personal air and heating controls for each passenger, since the client wants the passengers to have all kinds of comfort control at their fingertips.

LUXURY SEDAN

Now that you know what the client is looking for in a Luxury Sedan model, draw it out for them.

1

Draw a baseline using the ruler. Using the ellipses tool, draw the front wheel 1 in. off the baseline with B2 and B4. Draw the rear wheel 1 ⅛ in. (2.8 cm) off the baseline and 2 in. (5 cm) from the front tire. Use shapes B1 and B3 to draw the rear tire.

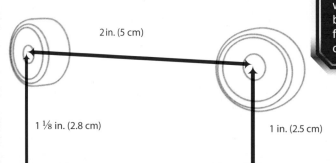

2 in. (5 cm)

1 ⅛ in. (2.8 cm)

1 in. (2.5 cm)

2

Draw simple shapes to show the basic outline of the car.

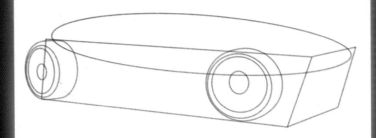

3

Refine the outline of the car using the curves and ellipses.

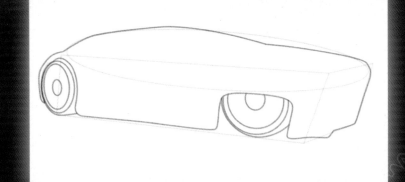

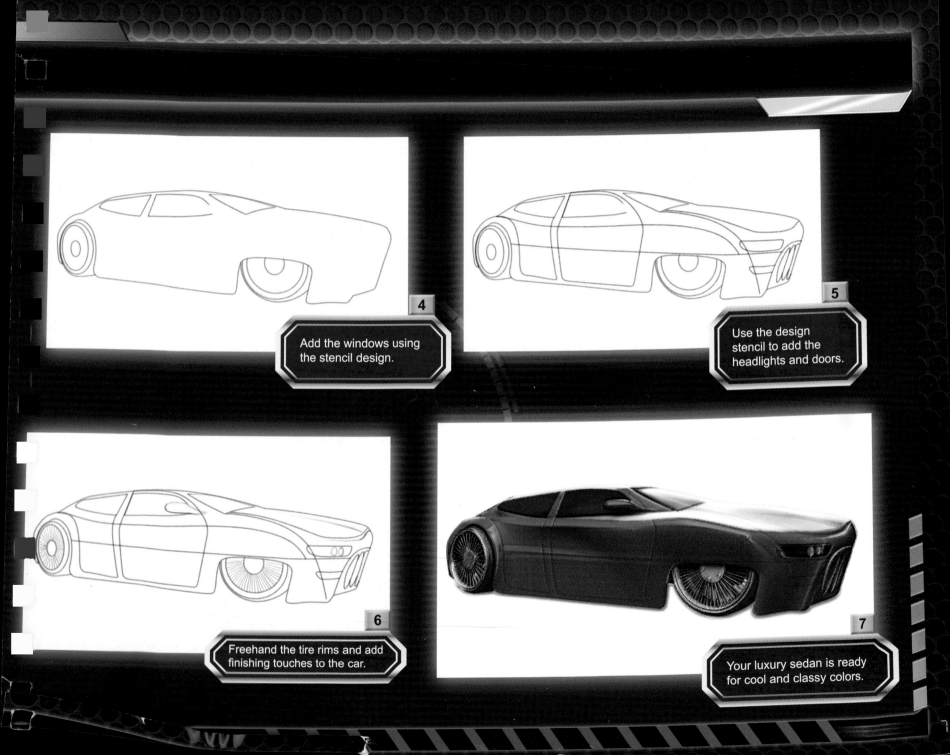

4 Add the windows using the stencil design.

5 Use the design stencil to add the headlights and doors.

6 Freehand the tire rims and add finishing touches to the car.

7 Your luxury sedan is ready for cool and classy colors.

HOVERCAPSULE

The car-manufacturing client is looking for a mix between a car and a plane. The car should be a two-seater with a lot of legroom and automated features including autopilot and GPS. The car should be eco-friendly, getting its power from photovoltaic cells on the back windshield.

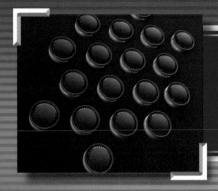

Sensitive photovoltaic cells on the roof and rear window of the car will power it even in low light.

The client would like a special glass for the windows and windshields that is light sensitive and helps reduce glare. The glass should also keep the car cool during hot days.

The vehicle should be able to hover 6.5 ft. (2 m) above the ground. And be able to reach speeds of 60 mph (96.5 kph) within 7 seconds.

The client wants comfort with a lot of legroom.

GPS and autopilot are a necessity for this client. Plug in your destination and kick back. Let the car do the driving.

HOVERCAPSULE

The car client has approved the initial concept of the car, so it's time to get started on the designs for the Hovercapsule. Let's go!

1

Draw the baseline using the ruler. The front wheel should be drawn 1 ½ in. (3.75 cm) from the baseline with C2 and C4. The back wheel will be ½ in. (1.25 cm) from the baseline and 1 ½ in. (3.75 cm) from the front tire with C1 and C3.

1 ½ in. (3.75 cm)

1 ½ in. (3.75 cm)

½ in. (1.25 cm)

2

Use the ruler and curves to make simple shapes to sketch the outline of the car.

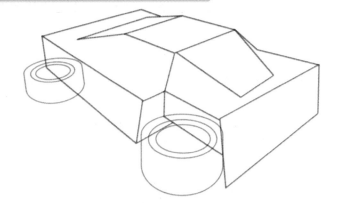

3

Use the curves tool to refine the basic shapes. Use the design stencil to draw the windows.

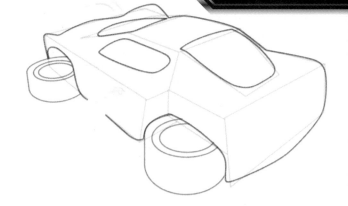

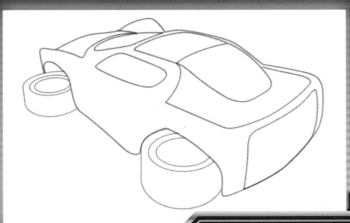

4 Use the design stencil to draw the roof and bumper.

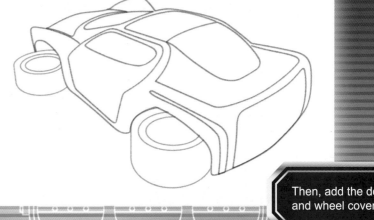

5 Then, add the door and wheel covers.

6 Add the details, including the photovoltaic cells, bumpers, door handle, and wheel trim.

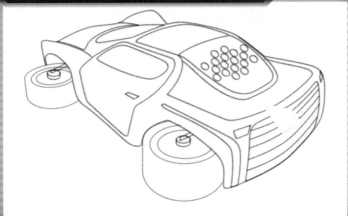

7 Color the Hovercapsule with cool metallic colors to make it look eco-friendly. Your client will love it.

SPORTS CAR

This car manufacturer wants the racing-car experience on the highway. It needs to be packed with features inspired by fighter jets. It needs to be fast and furious. Are you up for the task?

This supersporty car needs to be as comfortable as it is fast. And safety is of primary concern for this client.

The car must have an aerodynamic design to increase speed and keep the car on the ground.

Create a unique dashboard for the client, which will include GPS and thermal sensors to help avoid accidents at high speeds.

Trade out the regular steering wheel for twin-lever steering. This will give the driver more control.

The superpowerful engine should have 800 bhp (boiler horsepower) to reach the speeds the client wants.

SPORTS CAR

You know what the client wants. Now let's get to work on creating this sporty car.

1

Use the ruler to draw the baseline. To draw the front tire, use circle D2 and D4, ¾ in. (2 cm) off of the baseline. Measure 2 ½ in. (6.3 cm) from the front wheel and then 1 in. (2.5 cm) up to draw the back wheel using circle D1 and D3.

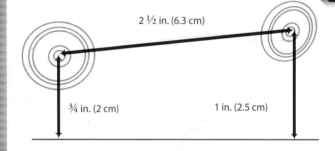

2 ½ in. (6.3 cm)

¾ in. (2 cm)   1 in. (2.5 cm)

2

Draw the outline of the car using simple shapes as shown.

3

Refine the outline using the curves tool.

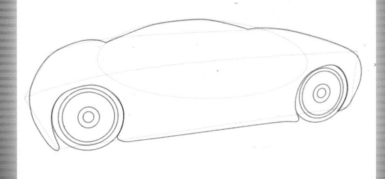

4 Use the design stencil to add the windshields and window.

5 Using the design stencil, add the doors, hood, thermal sensors, and wheel covers.

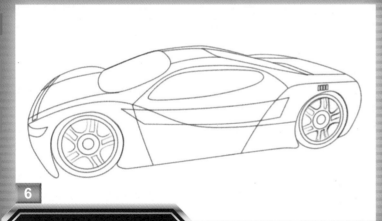

6 Now, add the wheel details using the design stencil.

7 Add color and highlights to your sports car.

CHAMELEON CAR

The client is a singing superstar, who would like a one-of-a-kind car that is uniquely his. He would like the outer skin to reflect his mood, favorite sports team, or to be invisible. This will be a tough one-- let's get started.

The client wants the car to be supercomfortable and stylish to reflect who he is.

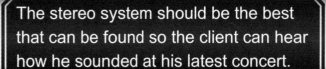

The stereo system should be the best that can be found so the client can hear how he sounded at his latest concert.

Use a new metallic "skin" for the body of the car. A computerized selection of images, specifically designed for the client, will display on the skin just like wallpaper on your computer or phone. A special mirror skin will reflect the surroundings, making the car invisible.

The car should have atmospheric air conditioning based on the outside air temperature and the client's preferred temperature.

The client wants nothing but luxury inside the car. It should feature plush leather seats with a custom seat for his dog.

CHAMELEON CAR

The singer is excited by your car ideas, so let's get drawing.

1

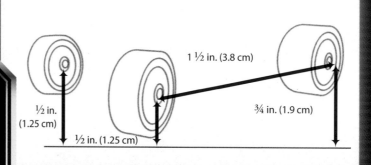

Use the ruler to draw the baseline. Draw the front right wheel using circle E2 and E4. Use circle E1 and E3 for the front left wheel and E5 and E6 for the back wheel. The front right wheel is ½ in. (1.25 cm) from the baseline. Now measure ½ in. (2.5 cm) from the right wheel to draw the left front wheel. Lastly, measure 1 ½ in. from the right front wheel to draw the back wheel, which is ¾ in. (1.9 cm) from the baseline.

2

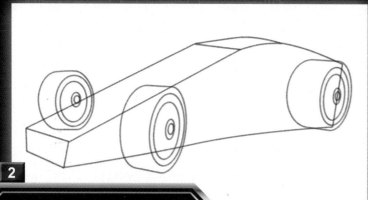

Use the ruler and curves to draw the simple shapes and outline of the car.

3

Use the curves tool to refine the simple shapes.

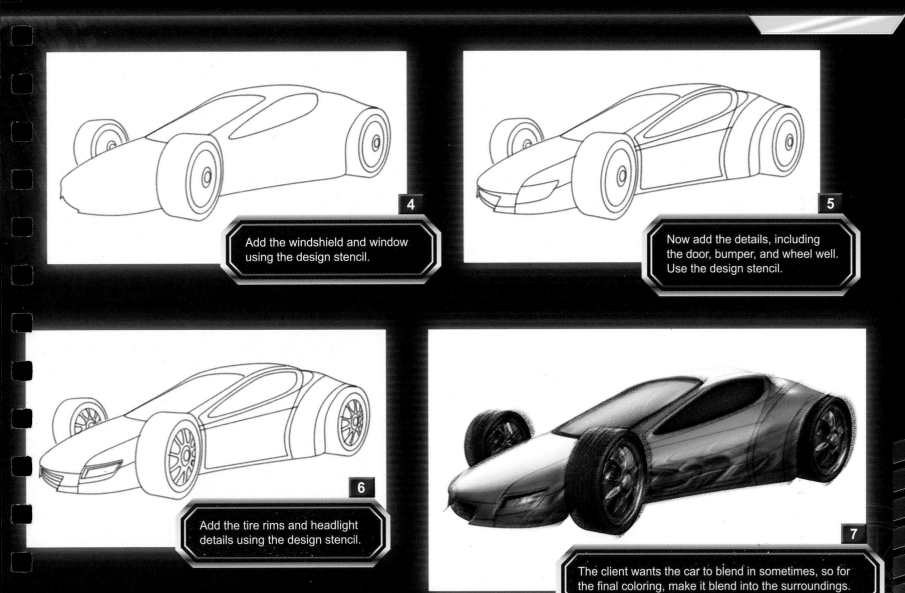

4 Add the windshield and window using the design stencil.

5 Now add the details, including the door, bumper, and wheel well. Use the design stencil.

6 Add the tire rims and headlight details using the design stencil.

7 The client wants the car to blend in sometimes, so for the final coloring, make it blend into the surroundings.

The Department of Transportation is looking for a new fleet of vehicles that can teach people to drive. Safety is the number one concern for this client, so there will be a lot of computer sensors and AI technology built in. This will be tricky, so let's get to work.

The client is very concerned with price, so the vehicle must be affordable to build.

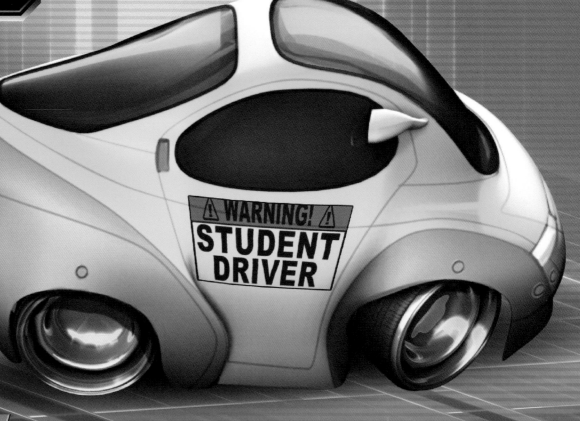

The onboard computer shows how well you are progressing and where you still need some work.

As the student becomes a better driver, the Artificial Intelligence technology lets the student manually control the vehicle.

Voice instruction and assisted steering will come standard with this vehicle.

The headlights on the car work as eyes for the Artifical Intelligence technology. It alerts the onboard computer of any dangers ahead that the driver may not be aware of.

Sensors all over the car, especially in the front and rear, allow the AI computer to take over the driving of the car if it senses any danger.

STUDENT DRIVER CAR

This client is looking for a safe car that teaches students how to drive and takes over when there is an emergency. Let's get to the drawing stage!

1

Draw the baseline with the ruler. On the far right of the line, draw a circle ½ in. (1.25 cm) from the baseline using F1 and F3 for the front wheel. For the back wheel, measure ½ in. up from the baseline and 1 ½ in. (3.8 cm) from the other wheel. Use circle F2 and F4 for the rear wheel.

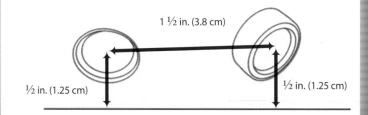

1 ½ in. (3.8 cm)

½ in. (1.25 cm)　　½ in. (1.25 cm)

2

Using the curves tool, draw the outline of the car using simple shapes.

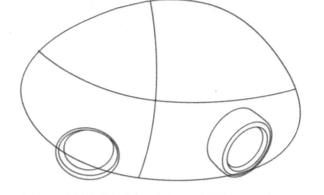

3

Refine the outline of the car using the curves tool.

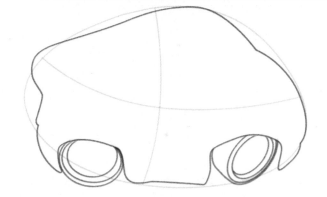

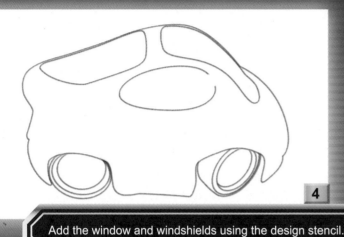

Add the window and windshields using the design stencil. **4**

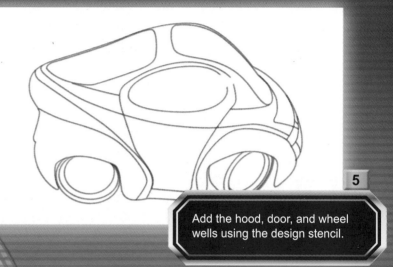

Add the hood, door, and wheel wells using the design stencil. **5**

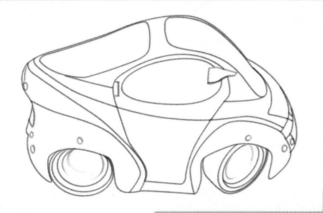

Now add the details and sensors. **6**

⚠ **WARNING!** ⚠
STUDENT DRIVER

7

Since the client wants to save money on these cars, the paint should be inexpensive. Add a different color where you think the sensors should go.

COUCH CAR

A sports superstar is looking for the ultimate ride. It should be the most comfortable vehicle and provide entertainment at the same time. He doesn't want a driver, but doesn't want to drive either. Your work is cut out for you. See what you can do.

With the futuristic design of the car, this superstar client will be the envy of all of his teammates.

This sports star wants to tell the car where to go and have it drive him there. The onboard navigation system and AI computer will be like his own chauffeur.

The wide wheel base keeps the car hugging the road even at high speeds.

This superstar's vehicle will need extensive computer programming and AI technology so he can kick back and enjoy the ride.

Comfort is extremely important to this client. Be sure to add plush seating, as well as a complete entertainment system.

COUCH CAR

All of the features in this vehicle are going to make it a tough job. Let's get drawing.

1

Use the ruler to draw a baseline. Draw the front wheel touching the baseline with the center ¼ in. (.63 cm) from the baseline using circles G2 and G4. Measure 1 ¼ in. from the center of the front wheel to the draw the back wheel. Measure ½ in. (1.25 cm) up from the baseline and use G1 and G3 circles.

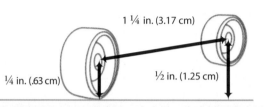

1 ¼ in. (3.17 cm)

¼ in. (.63 cm)   ½ in. (1.25 cm)

2

Use the ruler and curve to draw the simple shapes of the car.

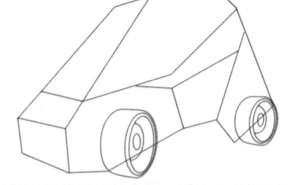

3

Refine the outline using the curves tool. Add the window and windshield using the design stencil.

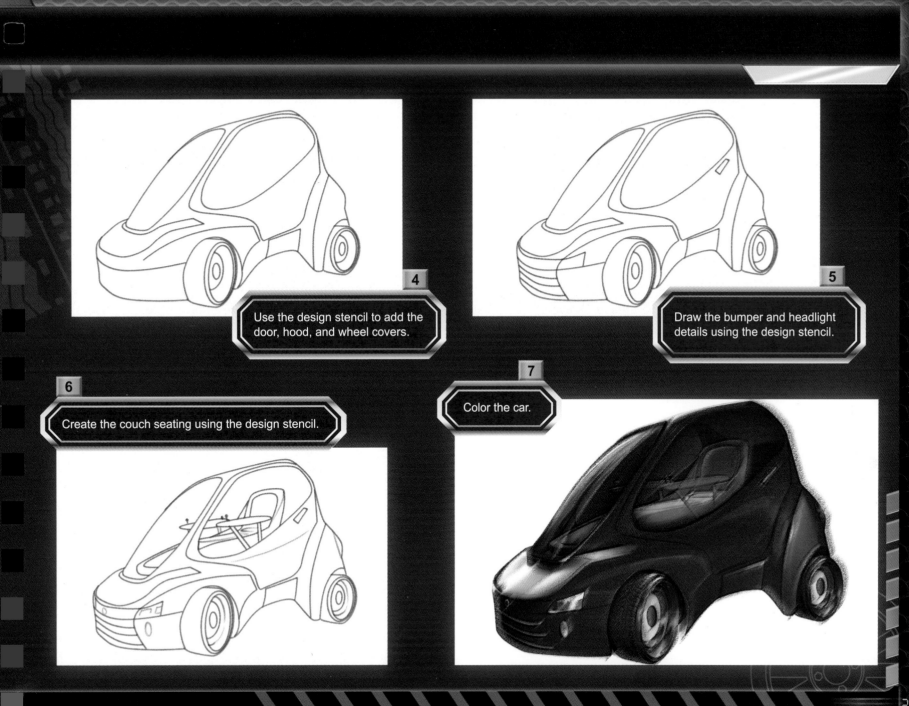

4 Use the design stencil to add the door, hood, and wheel covers.

5 Draw the bumper and headlight details using the design stencil.

6 Create the couch seating using the design stencil.

7 Color the car.

ARTIFICIAL INTELLIGENCE (AI) CAR

A large car manufacturer has come to you for the design of a supercompact and eco-friendly car design. It needs to be extremely safe and fuel efficient, so you should consider the new Artificial Intelligence technology. Let's get going.

The Artificial Intelligence brain is located within the dashboard. It is the Central Command Center of the car.

The Artificial Intelligence car comes with a name based on its personality. It's just like choosing a puppy!

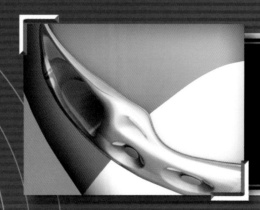

The headlights not only illuminate the road, but they are the eyes of the Artificial Intelligence brain. It sees 1,000 times better than you do in poor light conditions.

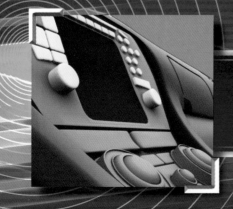

The car contains the latest voice recognition software. The doors on your Artificial Intelligence car open on your command and only your command.

ARTIFICIAL INTELLIGENCE (AI) CAR

Time is of the essence. You need to get this assignment done in a hurry. Break out your tools and let's get started.

Using A1, A2, A3, and A4 circles on the ellipses tool, draw two wheels at a distance of 1.2 in. (3 cm) from each other. Draw the front wheel ½ in. (1.25 cm) off of the baseline, while the rear wheel should be ¾ in. (1.9 cm) from the baseline.

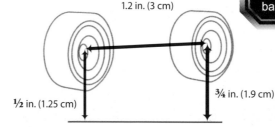

1.2 in. (3 cm)

½ in. (1.25 cm)

¾ in. (1.9 cm)

Draw simple shapes to show the basic outline of the car.

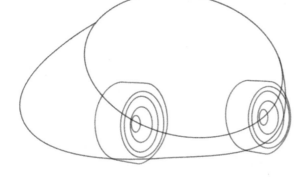

Refine the shapes using the curves tool. Now the car is taking shape.

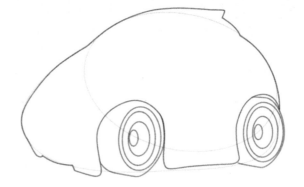

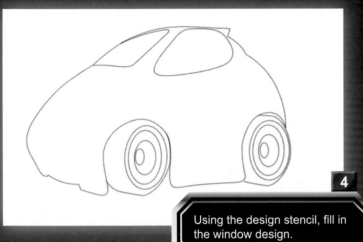

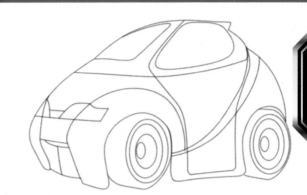

5 Using the design stencil, draw the headlights, door, wheel covers, and details.

4 Using the design stencil, fill in the window design.

6 Freehand the wheel rims and grille to add the finishing touches to the car.

7 Your AI car design is ready. Color the car in your favorite colors.

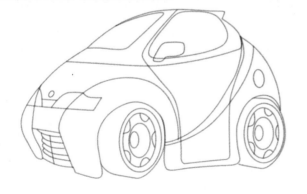

IT'S YOUR TURN

You've designed all kinds of cars for others. Now, design one for yourself. If you were going to create a car, what features would you want?

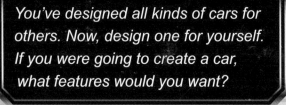

How about something like this All-Terrain vehicle that can move in any direction? You are well on your way to being an *awesome car designer!*